Ideas for Assemblies

Alan Millard

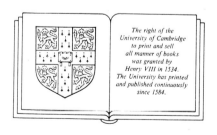

The right of the University of Cambridge to print and sell all manner of books was granted by Henry VIII in 1534. The University has printed and published continuously since 1584.

Cambridge University Press

Cambridge

New York   Port Chester   Melbourne   Sydney

Published by the Press Syndicate of the University of Cambridge
The Pitt Building, Trumpington Street, Cambridge CB2 1RP
40 West 20th Street, New York, NY 10011, USA
10 Stamford Road, Oakleigh, Melbourne 3166, Australia

First published 1990

Printed in Great Britain by Scotprint, Musselburgh, Scotland

British Library cataloguing in publication data

Millard, Alan
  Ideas for assemblies.
  1. Primary Schools. Morning assembly. Themes
  I. Title
  377′ .1

ISBN 0 521 38889 9

Contents

Contents

Foreword

Ideas for Assemblies is intended for those who do not have the time to read through long stories or track down reference material that might not be at hand. A consistent and simple format allows the user to see at a glance what is needed by way of preparation. The words in *italics* can be read as they are, or adapted to suit the circumstances. All of the ideas focus on personal–social themes that should appeal to children from widely differing backgrounds, and which lend themselves to supplementary stories and readings from other religions. The ideas aim to be

▶	complete in themselves	there are no references to other books
▶	concise and clear	each assembly follows a similar format
▶	practicable	the props suggested are found in many schools, and charts can be constructed from material already printed on the page
▶	participatory	children are involved
▶	multicultural	in the sense that they emphasise 'human' concerns common to various religions
▶	simple to use	in that most of the assemblies call for minimal preparation.

All of the assemblies have been used with children aged from 8 to 12.

Many hands make light work

Essential props
- ▶ PE bench or other heavy equipment
- ▶ A blackboard (without an easel) and chalk

Starting points

Who knows the saying, 'Many hands make light work'? What does it mean?
Listen to answers, ask for examples and discuss them.

Today we'll see if it's true. I need two volunteers to help me draw a plan on the blackboard.
Select two children, one to be the 'easel' and the other to watch what you draw on the blackboard.

ACTIVITIES

1. Ask one child to hold the blackboard high and still.

   After a struggle it will be quite clear that more help will be needed. Get additional helpers and make the point that many hands do seem to make light work.

2. Draw a plan to show how the second child must move a bench from one side of the hall to the other without disturbing any of the children. Ask the child to do it.

   After an initial struggle, more help can be enlisted in order to complete the task safely and successfully. The point that 'many hands make light work' can be made again.

Closing points

Do 'many hands make light work'?
Will it always be true?
(There could be a discussion on the idea, 'Too many cooks . . .'.)

Can anyone think of other jobs that would need a lot of help from several people?

Let's see if we can help today when something needs 'many hands'.

Too many cooks spoil the broth

Essential props
▶ Four pencils (two red and two blue)
▶ Two pieces of card
▶ Two tennis balls

Starting points

Who's heard of the saying, 'Too many cooks spoil the broth'? What does it mean?
Listen to explanations, ask for examples, discuss them.

Is it true that 'too many cooks spoil the broth'? How can we find out?

Let's try some experiments.

ACTIVITIES

1 Call two groups of children to the front:
(a) 12 children   (b) 2 children
Give two coloured pencils and a piece of card to one child from each group. Ask each group to design a birthday card with the instruction that every member of each group must contribute.

Impose a strict time-limit. Watch what happens, show everyone the results, and discuss them in the light of the saying, 'Too many cooks . . .'. Is the saying true in relation to the task?

2 Give one tennis ball to each group. Get each group to play 'catch'. Everyone in the group must be involved. The winners will be the group whose individual members make the greatest number of catches.

Decide on a time-limit. Watch what happens and discuss the results.

Closing points

Do 'too many cooks spoil the broth'?
Is it always likely to be true?

Depending on the age range, there might be some discussion on the opposite idea, that 'many hands make light work'.

See what happens today and ask yourselves, at different times, if there are 'too many cooks'.

Trust

Essential props
- ▶ A chocolate bar (or other reward) put in a predetermined place (e.g. Head's room)
- ▶ Eight so-called valuable 'obstacles' (e.g. vases placed on the floor in a line)
- ▶ A blindfold

Starting points
What do we mean when we say that we 'trust' someone? Has anyone 'trusted' someone today?
Discuss examples. Prompt if necessary, e.g. trusting parents.

ACTIVITIES

1 *Who would like a bar of chocolate?*
Send a volunteer to the wrong place. Wait for him or her to return emptyhanded and point out that on this occasion your word was not to be trusted.

2 Ask for another volunteer to come to the front. Explain that you want the volunteer to step over the line of 'precious' vases.

Let the volunteer do it once and then explain that you want it done blindfolded. You will act as 'guide'. When the volunteer is blindfolded, remove the obstacles – **silently**!

Guide the volunteer over the imaginary obstacles. Keep saying how precious they are, how near to being knocked over they are and how careful the volunteer must be.

At the end, remove the blindfold and share the joke.

3 Send the first volunteer to another place for the chocolate – this time the right place!

Ask the children what they think will happen.

Closing points
Celebrate the first volunteer's return – with the chocolate!
It pays to trust – even if we are let down, sometimes.

People sometimes *have* to co-operate

Essential props ▶ A hoop

Starting points

When do people need to co-operate?
Examples might include the following:

(a) A family dispute over which TV programme to watch
What can we do if several people want to watch different TV programmes at the same time?
Discuss possibilities: Weekly rota? Tossing for it? Video and save? Other options?

(b) Family holidays
How can families agree about where to spend their holidays?
Talk about ideas: Discuss and vote? One decides? Put a pin in a map? Other possibilities?

ACTIVITIES

1 Call two children to the front (centre). Explain that when you tell them to they are to walk at the same time to opposite sides of the hall, touch predetermined points (e.g. door and bench) and return to the centre.
Let them do it.

2 When they return, 'hoop' them together and ask them to do the same thing again – that is, separately, at the same time.

3 After a brief struggle, **stop them** and ask how they could touch both points – still hooped together. Invite suggestions.

4 When the children realise that they must go **together**, first to one point, then to the next, and finally back to the centre, let them do it.

Closing points

Some things can't be done unless we co-operate.
Let's try to co-operate whenever we can.

Mutual support

Essential props ▶ None

Starting points Who likes acting in front of an audience?
Question those who do in more detail. What do they like about it?
What can they do best? Are some things easier than others? How
would they feel about talking, acting, singing a solo or dancing?

Who doesn't like being on stage?
Explore their reasons. Draw attention to the contrasts between the
two groups. What happens to the worriers when they stand on
stage? How do they feel? What frightens them most?

How can we help a person who suffers from stage fright?
Listen to suggestions. Draw attention to the fact that it often helps
when two people work together and support each other.

Is there anyone here who wouldn't come out to the front alone but
would come with a friend?
Choose a volunteer, and let the volunteer choose a willing friend.

ACTIVITIES Some things are easier to do than others. Let's see what the
volunteer can do.

Begin with some simple questions. For example,
What's your name? Where do you live? Do you have any brothers or
sisters? What can you tell us about them?

Now, how would you feel if I asked you to do a 'slow dance'?
React supportively and then explain:
Not many people could do a slow dance, just like that, but this is
where a friend can help.
The volunteer is to move slowly while the friend 'mirrors' every
movement. They must both concentrate hard, keep exactly
together and make as many different shapes as they can.
Encourage and support all the time.

When the dance ends, question the volunteer:
Was it as difficult as you expected? What, if anything, made it
easier? Could you have done it without your friend?

Closing points When friends help us we can do much more than we think. Let's
encourage each other today by letting our friends help us, and by
helping them.

Team work or solo?

Essential props
▶ Large quantity of unsorted Cuisenaire rods
▶ A stopwatch or timer
▶ A table

Starting points
There are different ways of working in class. We can work alone, or in pairs, or in groups.
Who prefers to work alone? (Explore reasons.)
Who prefers to work as one of a pair? (Ask why and when.)
Who prefers to work in groups? (Ask for reasons and examples.)
Which is the best way of working?
Hear some answers. Who agrees – who disagrees – and why?
Encourage discussion and suggest that different tasks might lend themselves to different ways of working. For example,
What kinds of work are best done (a) alone? (Why?)
(b) in pairs? (Why?)
(c) in larger groups? (Why?)
Before we begin any task we could ask
(a) how many people will be needed?
(b) what should each person do?

ACTIVITIES
1 *First we'll sort out these Cuisenaire rods into groups, by colour. Let's begin with one person.*
Choose someone and let that person work for a timed period. Note how successful the result is and discuss it.

Let's do it again, but this time with two people – a pair.
Give them the chance to plan how they will do it and then repeat the task. When the time runs out, stop them, discuss the results and ask them how they planned their work.

Let's do it once more, but this time with a group.
Let the group plan its approach and begin. Discuss the results.

2 *Now we shall see who can build the tallest tower.*
Three towers are to be built – by the individual, by the pair and by the group – at the same time, on the table, over a timed period. Discuss the results at the end.

Closing points
Which way worked best for each of the tasks – and why?
Before you do anything today, think of the best way to do it.

A balanced team

Essential props
- ▶ A table and two chairs
- ▶ A stopwatch or timer
- ▶ Two pairs of scissors
- ▶ Pages from magazines or comics, with words printed on them
- ▶ Some quick-drying glue or paste
- ▶ Two sheets of plain card
- ▶ Two perfect circles drawn on separate sheets of paper

Starting points

Who likes TV quiz shows?
Choose some children to describe their favourite quiz shows and explain why they like them.

Who's taken part in a quiz?
Ask what kind of quiz, how well they did and how they felt.

What kind of person makes a good quiz-team member – someone who works quickly but not always accurately, or someone who works slowly and carefully?
Discuss suggestions, focusing on reasons for and against.

Is anyone here quick but careless?
Choose a willing volunteer to sit at the table.

Is anyone slow but careful?
Choose another volunteer to join the first one at the table. Thank both for taking part in what is to be the 'X' school assembly quiz.

ACTIVITIES

1 *In the first game the winner gets ten points, the loser none.*
Explain that the task is to cut out individual words from the torn-out pages and paste them on to the plain card to make a completely new sentence in a time-limit of 2 minutes. The longest sensible sentence (or start of a sentence) wins.

2 *In the second game the winner gets ten points, the loser none.*
Explain that the second task is to cut out the circle drawn on the paper. The neatest effort will win. (Give them as long as it takes – without telling them that there is no time-limit.)

Closing points

Are these the results we expected?
Do the people you mix with have different skills?
What skills would you bring to a quiz team? How do you know?

Believing in yourself

Essential props
- ▶ A tray with up to ten 'objects' on it
- ▶ A traycloth
- ▶ A picture with detail, e.g. a landscape

Starting points

Who enjoys tests? What do you like about them? Are you good at them?

Who doesn't like tests? What don't you like about them? Do you do well in them?

How many different kinds of test are there?
(Prompt: Subject tests? Cycling tests? Fitness tests? Others?)

What do you need to succeed in a test?
(Prompt: Skill? Knowledge? Stress the idea of **self-confidence**.)

ACTIVITIES

Select some volunteers to come out and memorise some of the objects on the tray. Cover up the tray and ask the volunteers to tell you what was on the tray. Tailor the task to suit the individual. Praise success.

As confidence grows, alter the activity. Ask volunteers to study the picture. When they've looked at it, turn it over and ask about various objects that were **not** in the picture. Make definite suggestions, e.g.
Was the dog brown or white? (when there was no dog)
Was the cottage thatched or tiled? (when there was no cottage)
What was the boy carrying? (when there was no boy)
Did the church have a tower or spire? (when there was no church)

When the activity is completed, congratulate any children who could not remember seeing some of the objects you said were there. Reveal your deception to those who said they saw them!

Closing points

Why did some say they saw things that weren't there? (Ask individuals.)
If we think someone knows more than us, do we lose confidence? How often do we keep quiet, or agree with people, just because they seem so sure of themselves?
Who's likely to keep quiet today when someone says something that doesn't sound true?

Let's all try to believe in ourselves enough to say what we think.

The whole truth?

Essential props   ▶ Newspaper page with a small hole torn through it
(Circle in red some statements that might not be strictly 'true',
e.g. advertisements for holidays.)

Starting points   *How do we know if something is 'true'?*

Pause after each of the following questions to discuss examples
of what children thought was true, at first, but later discovered
was not.
Do your friends always speak the truth?
Is what your parents tell you always 'true'?
Is everything you hear from teachers 'true'?
Is everything you see on TV 'true'?
Is everything you read in books 'true'?
Do newspapers always print the truth?

ACTIVITIES   **1** Ask for a volunteer (who can read) to come and sit with you
at the front in order to look at the newspaper. Offer the
selected page to the volunteer. Apologise for the 'hole', saying it
was the only newspaper you could find. Ask the volunteer to
describe what he or she sees. (Repeat what is said so that everyone
hears. Lead with questions if it helps.)

Draw the volunteer's attention to the 'ringed' statements and ask if
they are true. (e.g. Can any particular holiday resort 'have it all' –
Everest and Snowdon?) Open the discussion.

2 When the subject matter has been discussed for long
enough, ask for the newspaper yourself so that you can see
what is there.

Hold the newspaper in front of you and look around the hall –
peering through the hole. Describe what you see (through the
hole), mentioning children, staff and objects by name.

Closing points   *What do we mean when we say things are true? Different people
see different things. Can anyone ever know the 'whole' truth?*

Accepting people as they are

Essential props

▶ A duster
▶ A chair
▶ A piano (or something as heavy)
▶ A difficult music score

Starting points

How many of you like yourselves? Can you tell us why?
Select some replies.

How many of you don't like yourselves? Can you tell us why? What would you like to change?
Listen to some answers.

How are people different from each other? Think of some ways.
Encourage discussion on height, weight, colour of eyes or hair, etc. Emphasise that people are different from each other but not better or worse than each other.

ACTIVITIES

Today I need some help. Who can dust?
Select a volunteer and ask him or her to dust the ceiling (or anything out of reach). Offer a chair or suggest standing on tip-toe.
Eventually say (humourously), *X can't do it! He (or she)'s too short!*

Who is strong? I need someone to lift something for me.
Select two volunteers and ask them to lift the piano without moving it backwards or forwards. You can help them to position themselves, but eventually they must return to their places.
Make the point: *X and Y were much too weak.*

Who can play a tune on the piano?
Select a volunteer and, after letting them tinkle, ask them to play a difficult score from sight.
Make the point: *X was not clever enough to play it.*

Closing points

Was it right to blame these helpers for being too short, too weak or not clever enough?
Discuss each in turn.

*Let's ask our friends to do what they **can** do. We're all good at some things, and we all need to know what we're good at before we can 'like' ourselves.*

Knowing your limits

Essential props   ▶   Drum and drumstick
        ▶   A large thin book
        ▶   Pencil and paper
        ▶   Small table

Starting points   *What does it mean when someone says, 'Take one thing at a time'?*
Listen to answers.

When do we have to 'take one thing at a time'?
Encourage ideas, e.g. when we're doing too much at once.

Can anyone remember getting in a muddle by doing too much at once?
Hear examples. Ask what happened.

What would someone, who tries to do everything at once, do
– in a game of football?
– taking part in a project?
– during class lessons?
– learning something new like riding a bike or playing a recorder?

Why should we learn to 'take one thing at a time'?
(Prompt: To prevent errors? To do things properly?)

ACTIVITIES   *Let's see what happens when we **do** take one thing at a time.*
Ask for four volunteers.
Get one after the other to do each of the following activities:
(a) Beat the drum to a slow rhythm.
(b) Stamp to a slow rhythm.
(c) Balance book on head.
(d) Write name on piece of paper.
Praise each in turn.

Let's see what happens if we try to do too much at once.
Ask for one volunteer.
Starting with the first activity, build on each until the volunteer is trying to do **all four activities** at once.

Closing points   *What happened when the four volunteers did one thing at a time?*
What happened when one volunteer tried to do everything at once?
What can we learn about ourselves from what happened?

Facing up to fear

Essential props

▶ A large cardboard box filled with sawdust, sand or straw
▶ A prize of some kind (e.g. a wrapped lollipop) concealed in the sawdust

Starting points

We're all frightened by different things. What do you think would frighten most of us? How would you feel about
— being alone in the dark?
— meeting a wild animal?
— having to admit to something you'd rather keep quiet?
— being sent to the Head?
Tell children about your own childhood fears in order to step up the pace of discussion.

Who is brave enough to tell us about their own secret fears?
Listen to any offers, and comment supportively.

Who can remember getting over something that scared them once? Tell us about it.
Discuss the replies.

How do people get over their fears? Do they conquer them by
— growing out of them?
— facing up to them? How?

One of the best ways to overcome fear is to take a deep breath and face up to what really scares you. Who, for example, couldn't pick up a snake? Is one of you brave enough to have a go?
Encourage a volunteer to come out to the front.

ACTIVITIES

Explain that in the box you have a harmless snake which, because it comes from a warm country and likes to keep warm, has buried itself in the sawdust (or straw or sand).

Invite the volunteer to feel through the contents of the box, find the snake, and pick it up. **Stress that the snake is harmless**. Invite more volunteers if the first ones are too frightened, until one is 'brave' enough to attempt the challenge.

When the bravest one finds the 'reward', instead of the snake, hold it up for everyone to see and apologise for the white lie!

Closing points

Find out what frightens you most today and, if you can, work out what you can do to overcome the fear.

'Getting to know you'

Essential props ▶ Six chairs set out in a semicircle facing the assembly

Starting points

Everyone here is an individual. What does that mean?
Explore the idea of everyone being unique and having
– different backgrounds (families, homes, relations, beliefs)
– different histories (where they came from, what they've done)
– different personalities (cheerful, miserable, friendly, shy).
Ask for more ideas.

How do individuals get to know each other?
Talk about
– playing together or quarrelling with each other
– listening to and watching each other, in and out of school
– talking together
– asking questions
– any other ways.

We always have to work to get to know each other. Let's play a game that might tell us something new about someone.

ACTIVITIES

Ask for six volunteers, with good memories, to sit on the seats.
Explain the 'rules' so that everyone understands.

The children at the front will tell us their names, one by one. The first one says, for example, 'I am Tom.' The second one says, 'I am Mary and this is Tom.' The third one says, 'I am Jo, this is Mary and this is Tom', and so on until we've met them all.

When we've met them all they move on to the next stage: each one tells us his or her name and something he or she likes, for example 'I am Tom and I like dogs', then 'I am Mary. I like cats and Tom likes dogs', and so on.

After that we go on to the third stage by adding . . .

Continue as appropriate, suggesting more additions, e.g. dislikes, favourite colours, as much as the children can remember.

Closing points

Who learnt something new about someone?
How much do you know about your friends? Is there more to know?
Try to find out something new about one of your best friends today.

'My favourite things'

Essential props   ▶   Half-a-dozen chairs set out in a semicircle facing the assembly

Starting points   *I expect you've heard the saying, 'No two people are alike'. What does it mean?*
Accept all comments at first, but explain that you want to think, in particular, about people's likes and dislikes.

Would it be good if everyone liked the same things? If not, why not?
Consider various situations, e.g.
What would happen if everyone
— wanted to see the same football match?
— went to the beach every weekend?
— only liked travelling by train?
— only enjoyed reading books? (Who would write them?)
Invite the children to explore other possibilities of everyone liking the same things. Discuss their own likes and dislikes:
Who likes football? Who doesn't? Why? Why not? Who likes chess? (etc.)

Let's see what different people like most. I'll sit on this chair and show you what I like most. See if you can guess what it is.

ACTIVITIES   Sit on a chair and mime 'holding something you like' (e.g. a newspaper or a friendly cat), then ask:
What am I holding?

Invite the children to think of something they like and can hold, and, from those who can, choose six to come and sit at the front. Each child must mime 'holding something he or she likes' before passing it on to the next child who will, in turn, mime what he or she is holding, and so on.

When we've seen them all, we'll see who recognises and remembers them.

Closing points   *Was everyone holding the same object?*
What would happen if we did it again with a different group?
Is it true, do you think, that no two people are alike?
What do you know about your friends' likes and dislikes?
Do you know enough to know what presents they'd enjoy?

Taking a fresh look at an old problem

Essential props
- ▶ Blackboard, easel, chalk and cloth, or equivalent
- ▶ Six canes (of roughly equal length)

Starting points
Has anyone here ever started something, 'got stuck' and given up?
Can we have some examples?
Listen to examples, notice and discuss
— what makes people give up. (Difficulty? Boredom? Frustration?)
— which examples are common to most. (Maths? Jigsaw puzzles?)
— how people react when they get stuck. (Abandon? Try again?)

ACTIVITIES
Ask for three volunteers to solve the following problem.

Arrange six canes on the floor to make **four** *triangles. Each cane must form a* **complete** *side.*

Draw what they do on the blackboard so that all the children can see.

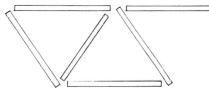

Example of plan of canes as laid out on floor

Other groups can be called out to solve the problem. If no group succeeds, the solution can be revealed: four triangles in **three dimensions**.

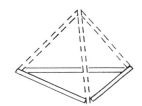

Dotted lines represent 'upright' canes

Demonstrate the solution. Three children can hold the ends of two canes at each of the corners (on the base triangle) while the teacher gathers together the three canes at the apex.

Closing points
What did we learn about tackling difficult problems?
(Seeing old problems from new angles? Trying different approaches?)
Could these ideas help us if we 'get stuck' today?
Could we use them when we 'get stuck' in playground arguments?

A fact is a fact (or is it?)

Essential props

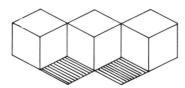

▶ The diagram illustrated here
(The diagram should be reproduced (enlarged on card) so that after it has been used with the volunteers, it can be shown to the whole school.)

Starting points

People say, 'A fact is a fact – you can't argue with the facts!'
*A judge might say, 'We must look at the facts'. But what **are** facts?*
Discuss replies. Get examples of 'facts' from the children.

Is there a difference between fact and fiction? What is 'fiction'?

Listen to these statements: which are facts and which are fiction?
– Without a telescope we can see about 3000 stars at night.
– 'The night has a thousand eyes,' [Poem 'Light' by
F.W. Bourdillon]

– A rose is a flower.
– 'O, my luve is like a red, red rose' ['A red, red rose' by
Robert Burns]

– Tigers have stripes.
– 'Tyger! Tyger! burning bright' ['The Tyger' by William Blake]

The point can be made that whereas poetry uses figures of speech that are not strictly true, scientific statements try to be accurate. For example,
If I say I'm boiling, do I mean that my blood is 100 degrees Centigrade? Scientists only deal with facts: they observe, measure and count. But can we always believe our eyes?

ACTIVITIES

Let some volunteers come to the front to count how many 'cubes' they can see on the card. Stand those who see three on one side, and those who see two on the other side.

Closing points

Are there two cubes or are there three?
Point out that it depends on whether the shaded parts are seen as the shadows of three white cubes, or as the bases of two cubes. Pause to let children see what you mean, or turn the card upside down.

Are there two cubes or are there three?

*What is a **fact**? Can we be sure that anything is a fact?*

Seeing is believing

Essential props
- ► A pen
- ► A pencil
- ► A one-pound coin
- ► A chair
- ► An enlarged version of the picture on this page

Starting points
Hold up a pen.
Who can tell me what this is? (Accept correct answer.)
Hold up a pencil.
Who knows what this is? (Accept right response.)
How do we know that this is a pencil and that this is a pen?
We know because we can see.

Would we believe a friend who said
– her father was a policeman?
– he had a swimming-pool in his back garden?

What would we need to do before we could be sure? (See for ourselves?)

ACTIVITIES

1 Invite a volunteer to come to the front, take the pound coin from the chair and return to his or her place. Call out six children (including the 'culprit'), to form an 'identity parade', and find out which one is 'guilty' by a show of hands. How do they know? (Because they **saw**!)
Retrieve the coin. Send the children back to their places.

2 Ask *Is this a pound coin or a gold sovereign?*
Invite some out to **see**, and **say** what they see.

3 *So – seeing is believing – but is it?*
Invite several children out, one at a time, to look at an enlarged version of the picture. Stand those who tell you it is a vase or candlestick on one side, and those who say it is two faces on the other side. Afterwards get them to say what they saw. Finally, show the school the picture.

Closing points
Can we always be certain that what we see is true? There are often at least two ways of looking at the same thing. Discuss examples: blaming particular people, making assumptions.
*Should we think twice before saying that we know **for certain**?*

Solving impossible problems

Essential props
- ▶ Blackboard, easel, chalk and cloth, or equivalent
- ▶ Two glasses, both half-filled with squash
  (Note: One glass must be small enough to fit inside the other)
- ▶ A table
- ▶ An empty washing-up bowl

Starting points

There is usually more than one way to solve a problem. For example, who can think of at least two ways to
– find a nail in a bucket of sand? (Finger through it? Use a sieve?)
– get something down from a tree? (Use a ladder? Throw a stick?)
– dry the dishes? (Use a teatowel? Let them drain? Any more examples?)

There are often different ways of solving the same problem. When a problem 'beats' us, can we find new ways to solve it?

ACTIVITIES

Ask volunteers to solve these problems.

Draw nine dots on the blackboard in 3 × 3 square formation (diagram A).

Problem 1: Link all the dots with four straight lines. Every line must lead on to the next. The chalk must never be lifted from the board (diagram B).

Let the volunteers try, one at a time. After a few attempts, a solution – if it has not been discovered – can be revealed (diagram C). It should be stressed that the solution is found by thinking 'beyond the dots themselves'.

Problem 2: Drink squash from one of the glasses without tilting it. Suggest that this is tried over the bowl in case of spillage! A solution, if not discovered, is found by placing the smaller glass into the larger glass and drinking the 'overflowing' squash.

Closing points

Today we'll all meet various problems – quarrels, losing things, being misunderstood. (Ask what problems the children expect to meet.) ***Don't give up!*** *Try to think of new ways to solve them.*

Rash judgements

Essential props ▶ Two ordinary boxes, one larger than the other, but each with similar prizes (e.g. lollipops) inside. The larger one must be gift-wrapped. The other should be left as it is.

Starting points

If you saw one man driving a Rolls Royce and another man cycling, which would be the rich one?
Note the responses but make no comment.

If you saw a lady sweeping up in a café, and another lady teaching at a school, who would be the clever one?
Note the responses again, but this time question the children:
Who thought the man in the Rolls Royce would be richer than the cyclist? Why? Does anyone disagree? Why? Who was clever   the cleaner or the teacher?
Continue reviewing the responses without adding your own view.

Some think one thing and others think something else. What more would we need to know about all four people before we could answer the questions?
Encourage ideas, underlining the fact that there is not enough information about the characters to make any judgements.
The cyclist might be a millionaire trying to keep fit.
The Rolls Royce driver might be the cyclist's chauffeur.
Can anyone think of a story about the teacher and the cleaner to explain why the cleaner might have been the clever one?
We need to know a lot before we can make up our minds about anything. Look at this problem.

ACTIVITIES

Hold up the two boxes. Ask which box has something nice in it. Notice who opts for which box. Choose a volunteer from each 'camp'.

Ask about the reasons for their choices and invite comments. Decide by a show of hands which box should be opened first. When the box has been opened, congratulate the 'winner'. Afterwards let the 'loser' look in his or her box.

Closing points

Never jump to conclusions.
Things aren't always the way they seem.
We shouldn't make too many judgements when we don't know enough.
Can we ever know enough?

Using the imagination

Essential props

▶ A picture of someone doing something
(Any picture will do. Leonardo da Vinci's 'Mona Lisa' is used here purely for illustrative purposes.)
▶ Two stacking chairs

Starting points

There can be more than one way of looking at the same thing. Look at this picture. What (in the case of the 'Mona Lisa') *is the lady doing?*
Accept the obvious explanation (the lady is looking at us).

Now let's use our imagination to think up some different explanations. For example, I could say that she is scratching her wrist or feeling her bracelet. Who can think of other explanations?
(Holding on to her severed hand? Hiding something?)
What is she thinking about?
(A tickle? Something she's lost? A hard sum? Something else?)

If we use our imagination we often see all kinds of possibilities.
Hold up the chairs.
Who can tell me what these are?
Accept the obvious answer at first, but then continue:
I want you to use your imagination. What else could they be?

ACTIVITIES

Call for volunteers, singly or in pairs, to think of what the chairs might be, before acting out a 'sketch' so that others can guess what they are. The chairs can be placed in any position. For example, in the upright position they might be seats in a vehicle, a horse, a piano, a computer, etc. Laid on their backs they might be seats in a spaceship, a barrier or partition. (Where?) They could be inverted, laid end to end, or moved into other positions. Praise every unusual idea that the children act out.

Closing points

By using our imagination we can see all kinds of different possibilities in everyday sights.
Try using your imagination as you look around today.
Can you change the way that you look at things, or even, perhaps, the way that you look at people? Do you have too many set ideas?

Mirror, mirror!

Essential props
- ▶ A photograph of yourself, or of someone else who will be at the assembly, would be useful, but not essential
- ▶ Some paper
- ▶ A pen or pencil
- ▶ A table
- ▶ A mirror (shaving-mirror size)

Starting points

Who knows what they look like?
Where have you seen yourself?
How many different ways are there of seeing ourselves?
Suggest different ways, e.g. mirrors, paintings, drawings, photographs.

Are there any other ways?
How did the 'Ugly Duckling' find out she was a swan?
Will someone's photo be the same as their reflection?
Of those who don't think so, ask why, then explain:
Reflections make our right sides seem like our left sides — and vice versa. Hair partings, in reflections, are always on the 'wrong' side.
At this point a photograph — if there is one — could be used in conjunction with the mirror to convince the doubters.

What would our lives be like if we lived them only through mirrors?
Let's find out!

ACTIVITIES

Select children, one at a time, to come to the table and write their names, large enough for the rest to see, on the paper provided. Explain that they must write it first in the usual way, sitting at the table. Then they must write it again by looking up at the mirror and not at the paper. The mirror must be held **above** their heads. Discuss the results as they appear.

Closing points

Notice how mirrors distort our judgement!
If you want to know what you're really like, don't ask yourself.
Ask someone else.

Destroying and repairing

Essential props
- ▶ An old piece of china
- ▶ A table
- ▶ A newspaper
- ▶ A hammer
- ▶ A tube of glue

Starting points

Some people seem to like destroying things.

Who has had something destroyed by someone?
Discuss cases.

What can we destroy apart from 'things'?
Discuss ideas: friendships – trust – beliefs – hopes. Get the children to give examples of how they can be destroyed.

Sometimes it's fun to 'destroy' things. Who would like special permission to destroy something now?
Choose a volunteer!

ACTIVITIES

1 With the volunteer at your side, hold up the piece of china. Wrap it up in the newspaper and place it on the table. Give the volunteer the hammer and let it be used. Make sure that the article is well and truly destroyed.

Ask the volunteer how it felt!
Was it easy?

2 Explain that you still need the volunteer to help you. Unwrap the newspaper so that everyone sees what has happened. Can anyone guess what you'll ask the volunteer to do?

Spread the newspaper (with its contents) out on the table. Give the volunteer a tube of glue. Ask the volunteer to repair the piece of china.

Closing points

Which is easier, destroying things or repairing them?
Is it the same with friendships?

Choices

Essential props
- ▶ Two pieces of drawing paper
- ▶ Two packets of crayons
- ▶ Two tables, one on each side of the hall

Starting points

Every day we have to make choices. What choices do you have to make when
– it's time to get up, and someone calls you?
– a friend turns up and asks you to come out?
– it's a wet Saturday morning?
– your teacher has to go out of the classroom and leave you?
– you get home, the house is untidy, and no one is in?
– you're bored and there's nothing to do?

Who can remember making a choice today?
Discuss examples and ask, of each:
– What was the choice?
– Did you make the right decision?
– Why?/Why not?
– Were other choices possible?

Are some choices easier to make than others?

ACTIVITIES

Ask for four volunteers and divide them into two pairs. Suggest to the school that each pair will be able to choose what to do with the paper and crayons – but whisper, to the first pair, that you want a good coloured picture of a flower, drawn quickly, and to the second pair that you want a page of scribble. (The deception can be explained later.) Encourage the pairs as they work, on separate tables, with their backs to the school.

Hold up the finished results and ask:
Which pair made the best choice? Why?

After discussion, explain what really happened, and your part in it.

Closing points

One choice led to something quite pointless; the other had a purpose.
Let's notice what choices we get today – and what we do with them!

Optimistic or pessimistic?

Essential props
- ▶ An enlarged copy of the picture on this page
- ▶ A glass half-filled with water (or squash)
- ▶ Two children already primed with answers (see Activities below)

Starting points

We often see the same thing in different ways. Look at this!

Show everyone an enlarged version of the picture, and ask:
What is it?
Who sees an old lady?
Who sees a young woman?

Some time can be spent pointing out that the 'old lady' is looking towards them whilst the 'young woman' is looking away. Indicate points of correspondence, e.g. nose – cheekbone; eye – ear; mouth – neck.

I wonder if sad people see an old face and if cheerful people see a young face! Whether they do or not, we often describe cheerful people as **optimists** *and miserable people as* **pessimists***.*
An optimist looks on the 'bright' side of life. A pessimist always expects the worst.
What might an optimist do
– when something goes wrong? (Get examples from the children.)
– when faced with a problem? (e.g. a puncture or a broken toy)
– when given bad news? (e.g. a cancelled holiday or treat)
What might a pessimist do in the same situations? (Repeat them.)

ACTIVITIES

Look at this glass of water (or squash). Two children are coming out to tell us what they see.

Call out the two children, one primed to say, 'I see a glass half-full,' and the other primed to say, 'I see a glass half-empty.'

Closing points

Which one was optimistic? Why?
Discuss ideas, e.g. looks forward, expects more pleasure, etc.
Which one was pessimistic? Why?
Discuss ideas, e.g. looks back, is full of regret, etc.

Let's try to notice when we are being optimistic or pessimistic.
Can we be optimistic when others aren't?

Creating a muddle and sorting it out

Essential props
- ▶ Separate quantities of sugar and salt
- ▶ A transparent container

Starting points

What do people do when they 'mess things up'?
(Spoil things? Break rules? Act 'stupidly'?) Discuss ideas.

How would someone 'mess up'
– a game? (Get specific examples.)
– a lesson? (Be careful to avoid specific examples!)
– a birthday party? (Encourage different ideas.)
– a school visit? (e.g. By getting lost?)

Explain how easy it is to spoil something that has been organised by not 'keeping to the rules' – and how difficult it can be to sort something out when someone makes a mess of it (e.g. saying the wrong line in a play, taking home the wrong coat, or losing a note from school). Ask for more examples.

ACTIVITIES

1 Show the children the sugar and the salt and ask, of each:
What is it?
Where does it come from? (Mines, plants?)
How is it used? (Making cement/glass? Cooking?)
Could either be used in the place of the other?
How can we tell which is which?

Ask for two helpers and get each to guess which is which by
– looking. (Ask them to describe the different textures.)
– feeling. (Let them hold samples and say how each feels.)
– tasting. (Can they say how each one tastes?)

2 Ask them how they could 'muddle them up'!
Let them do it by mixing them in the container.
Ask how the mixture looks, feels and tastes.

3 Ask them to separate the ingredients!

Closing points

Can the mixture be used for cooking or making cement any more?
Which is easier: muddling things up, or sorting them out?

Looking on the bright side

Essential props
▶ A table
▶ Paper
▶ A pencil
▶ Paints, brushes and water

Starting points

Some people always 'look on the bright side'.
What does 'looking on the bright side' mean?
Listen to suggestions and help with specific questions:
What would people who 'look on the bright side' do
– at the seaside when it pours with rain?
– when they break something precious?
– when they lose all their savings?

What would people who look on the 'black side' do?
Repeat the same questions and comment on responses.

Has anyone had a disappointment today? What happened?
Encourage the children to talk about real experiences and ask them
how they reacted. Did they look on the bright side?

Let's imagine a situation. I need a volunteer who can draw and paint.
Invite a volunteer to sit at the table.

ACTIVITIES

Draw a circle and paint exactly inside it.
Encourage the child at every stage. Describe what is happening and
praise the care that goes into the work. As soon as the child is
painting up to the line, jog the table (accidentally of course) and
apologise profusely. Show the painting to the children.

Look what has happened! Has anyone ever been in a similar
situation? What would we do now, if we look on the 'black side'?
Listen to suggestions.

What could we do if we looked on the 'bright side'?
Encourage positive responses, e.g. *Could we*
– enlarge the circle?
– use the mistake? How?
Get as many ideas as possible and, if there's time, give the artist a
chance to take corrective action.

Closing points

Notice how you react when something goes wrong.
Try to 'look on the bright side' and make the best of it.

Either or both?

Essential props	▶ White paper with a shape drawn on it (see diagram A)
	▶ Black paper (more than twice the size of the white paper)
	▶ Scissors
	▶ Paste and applicator
	▶ Table

Starting points

Who can describe a 'good' person?
Encourage a discussion on what makes a person 'good'.

Who can describe a 'bad' person?
Discuss what makes someone 'bad'.

Is anyone 'good' or 'bad' all the time?
Through more discussion suggest that no one is 'good' or 'bad'.
Most of us are both   sometimes 'good' and sometimes 'bad'.

We could say 'there are two sides to every coin'. What does that mean?
Examine the idea of opposites, e.g.
— *Could there be darkness without light?*
— *Could we be happy if we weren't ever sad?*
— *Could we feel well if we never felt ill?*
Ask the children to think of similar examples.

We often like to forget the 'bad' things, but life includes everything, good and bad. If we can, we should make use of everything.

ACTIVITIES

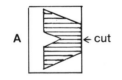

Who is fairly good at cutting out shapes?
Choose a volunteer, and give him or her the piece of white paper.
Cut out the shaded 'V' but don't throw the waste away. Keep both pieces.

We often throw away the waste (like the bad things that happen in life), but instead we'll make use of it. Watch what happens.

Instruct the volunteer:
Paste both the shaded shape and the cut-away surround to the black paper.

Closing points

If we make use of everything, everything is useful!
*Let's try to make use of whatever happens today, the good **and** the bad.*

Can I or can't I?

Essential props ▶ Two chairs

Starting points

People can be cheerful, or miserable. They can make us feel good, or feel bad.

How do the people who make us feel good behave? How would they act towards someone
– who's in a bad mood?
– who feels embarrassed?
– who's been successful at something?
– who gets into trouble?
– who comes to school in new clothes?
– who changes his or her hairstyle?

How would people who make us feel bad behave in the same situations?
Discuss the same situations again and encourage ideas.

How do we affect other people? Do we make them feel good or bad? Let's try an experiment with two people.

ACTIVITIES

Ask for two volunteers who would be willing to answer some questions about themselves. Invite them to sit on the chairs.

Ask the first child some negative questions, e.g.
What do you hate most about yourself?
What are you worst at?
What can other people do better than you?
What don't teachers like about you?
What annoys your parents about you?
What are your worst subjects at school?
Do you feel good about yourself after answering my questions?

Turn to the second child and ask for positive replies:
What is the best thing about your looks?
What do you like most about yourself?
What are you good at?
What do teachers like about you?
What do your parents like about you?
What are you best at in school?
How do you feel after answering these questions?

Closing points

Notice what makes you feel good.
Do something to make someone else feel good.

'Warm' behaviour and 'cold' behaviour

Essential props

▶ Two glasses, one filled with cold water and one with very warm water (If it can be arranged, it might be better to have the warm water brought in later.)
▶ A jar of coffee (granules are best)
▶ A spoon

Starting points

What is the difference between a 'warm' person and a 'cold' person?
What do the two descriptions mean? Give me some examples of what
— a 'warm' person is like. (Listen, encourage discussion, comment.)
— a 'cold' person is like. (Listen again, discuss and comment.)

Aesop wrote a fable, about the cold north wind and the warm sun, that has something to do with warm and cold behaviour. Who knows the story? In the fable the wind challenges the sun by saying, 'I'll bet I can make that traveller take off his coat before you can'. The wind tries, but nothing happens — except that the man wraps up even more. But the sun, by shining, warms the man and before long he takes off his coat.

Encourage comment on the story, e.g. Is warm, gentle persuasion better than cold, brute force? Relate ideas to the following illustration.

ACTIVITIES

When we act 'warmly' towards people, we can make it easier for them to join our group. If the people in a school create a 'warm' atmosphere, visitors or newcomers feel 'at home'. They find it easier to mix with us.

Watch what happens when I put coffee into cold water. (Demonstrate.) *The coffee floats and then sinks. It doesn't mix with cold water. What will happen if I use hot water?* (Demonstrate.) *The water soon starts to turn brown. Coffee seems to like warm water.*

Closing points

Think of the warm things we like: a warm day, swimming or washing in warm water, warm baths, warm homes, warm clothes and warm beds, a warm welcome from strangers.

Does our school have a warm atmosphere?
What can we do to make sure that it does?

A problem shared is a problem halved

Essential props
▶ A small table
▶ Two wrapped sweets (or lollipops)

Starting points

Who knows the saying 'A problem shared is a problem halved'?
What does it mean?
Encourage answers and comment on them. Elicit ideas with
questions, e.g.
 — *Who's been in a 'jam'? What happened? How did you get out*
 of it?
 — *Has anyone helped someone out of a 'jam'? What kind of 'jam'?*
 What did you do to sort it out?
 — *Who remembers being asked to do something that needed help?*
 — *Can you think of times when at least two people are needed?*
 (Team games? Chess? Throwing a life-belt to a drowning man?)

Aesop tells the story of a boy who swims out of his depth and is
struggling to survive. A passing man calls out and tells him how silly
he is to get into such a mess.
Will that help the boy? What does he need from the man?

ACTIVITIES

Select a volunteer to come to the front, unwrap a sweet and eat it.
When the volunteer is there, explain that **hands** are to be **clasped
behind the back**!
Put the sweet on the table and let the attempt begin.
After a short time choose a second, unrestricted, volunteer to 'help'
the first one. When the task is accomplished, reward them both!

Closing points

We all need help, and we need to help others.
Let's try to lend a hand when people need our help today.
There are sure to be times when we shall need their help.

Confusing people

Essential props ▶ Three charts (see diagrams on this page)
▶ A metre rule

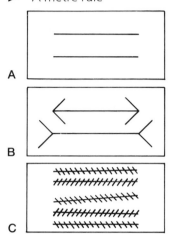

A

B

C

Starting points *Some people are straightforward. Others often confuse us.*

How do straightforward people behave?
Encourage ideas: Say what they mean? Mean what they say? Tell the truth? Give honest answers? Keep to their word?

How do people who 'confuse' behave?
Get more examples: Say one thing and mean another? Never do what they say they will do? Hinder more than they help? When? How?

ACTIVITIES *Look how easy it is to confuse something simple.*

Show chart A. Discuss ideas like 'parallel' and 'equal length'.

Show chart B. Are the lines still equal in length? Get opinions. Let children measure them. Point out how the 'arrows' confuse.

Show chart C. Explain that only **two** of the lines are parallel. Which two? Let children come to guess, then to check with the ruler. Why is it difficult to be sure? Stress again that the crossed lines confuse.

Closing points *Things are much simpler when they aren't confused.*
Do we confuse other people, or are we straightforward?
Let's notice how others react to us. Their reactions will tell us if we're being straightforward or not!

Listening to each other

Essential props   ▶ A variety of percussion instruments, e.g. triangle, drum, tambourine, cymbal, shaker

Starting points   *What happens when too many people talk at once?*
Listen to answers, and ask for examples of situations, e.g.
— answering questions in class;
— working together on a play;
— organising a game.

Why should children raise their hands in class?
Encourage as many ideas as possible, e.g.
— lets one person speak at a time;
— gives others the chance to listen;
— gives everyone a chance to have a say.

What would happen if everyone answered at once?
Discuss the implications: chaos — no one hearing — nothing but noise.

When people don't listen to each other, anything can happen. Let me show you what I mean.

ACTIVITIES   Share out the instruments — one to each volunteer — and say:
Play whatever you like, as loudly as you like, until I ask you to stop.
Let them play for a while, then stop them. Ask the other children:
Were they listening to each other? Were they working together? Did anyone take any notice of anyone else? What happened?

Let's try again, but this time in a planned way so that everyone listens to the rest and fits in with them.

Organise a plan, directing and suggesting as appropriate, e.g.
(a) Let one instrument start by repeating a catchy rhythm as a basis for building patterns. Rhythms of people's names could be used, e.g. Oliver and Mary — Oliver and Mary — Oliver and Mary, etc.
(b) Other instruments can join in, one at a time, with compatible rhythms, some on the strong beat, some on the weak beat, some playing most of the time, others only occasionally.
(c) Towards the end the instruments can drop out, one at a time, in reverse order, until only the first one to start is left playing.

Was there a difference? How was it different — and why?

Closing points   *People, like instruments, can work together if they notice each other. How will you join in, today? Will you talk and listen, or only talk?*

'Holding on' by 'letting go'

Essential props ▶ None

Starting points

What are 'possessions'?
Encourage ideas, e.g. things we own, things that are special, things that belong to particular people.

Who has a favourite possession?
Where do you keep it? Would you share it?

Can we possess people? Can we own our friends?

What happens if we try to keep friends to ourselves?
Promote discussion: have people lost friends through trying to keep them? How many people feel jealous when their 'best friends' get friendly with other people?

We're all possessive at times. Let's see what happens when we are –
and when we aren't. I shall need two volunteers to begin with.
The volunteers will have to be selected with care.
It might be advisable, in some schools, to choose the youngest children, particularly if the older ones would be inhibited by being asked to hold hands.

ACTIVITIES

Ask the first two volunteers to face each other and join hands (both using both hands).

Imagine these are two friends. Can either of them hold hands with anyone else? (Why not?)
If they only face each other, will they see anyone else? (Why not?)
They're stuck with each other. Is that good?
Let's see what happens if we try a different arrangement. Instead of facing each other, we'll ask them to hold hands standing side by side.
Make sure that each child has one hand free.
Because they have a free hand each, they can both choose another friend.
Let them choose two more to join them – one on each side.
How many are there in the group now? Can we have any more?
Two more can be invited to join hands at each end of the chain. The process can be repeated until the point has been made.

Closing points

By allowing our friends to have their own friends, friendships grow.
Think about your own friendship groups. Is there room for more?

Supporting friends

Essential props   ▶   Two large PE mats, laid end to end

Starting points

What do we mean by the word 'support'?
What supports
— a suspension bridge?
— the ceiling above us?
— an arch?
Encourage discussion on forms of support.

Buildings and structures need support — and so do people!
What supports a person with
— a broken arm? (Plaster? A sling?)
— a broken leg? (Crutches?)
— ageing limbs? (A walking frame? Walking sticks? A wheelchair?)

Do people need support in other ways?
Move towards the idea of 'emotional' support.
How can we support people who are
— lonely?
— sad?
— overworked?

Everyone needs some support at times. But if we want to be
supported we have to trust other people.

Can I have some trusting volunteers? I need thirteen!
Choose them.

ACTIVITIES

You will have to trust me, but it is safe — if you do exactly as I say.
Everyone in the room must be still so that no one is distracted.
Divide twelve of the volunteers into two groups of six. Each group
must mirror the other, kneeling up on the mats, next to each other,
shoulder to shoulder, close together, facing the other group. The
opposite partners (from each group) must link up by gently holding
each other's arms, just in front of the elbows, to form a 'mattress'
or 'bed' of arms, with no gaps. The 'thirteenth' person is asked to:
Dive, head first, on to the bed of arms! Don't be afraid to dive to the
end of the 'bed'.
The supporters must stay quite still and not give way when the diver
lands. They will be surprised at how lightly he falls.

Closing points

Do you trust your friends enough to let them support you?
Would you have the courage to support your friends?

How much do we hear?

Essential props
- ▶ Two small tables and chairs
- ▶ Paper and a pencil on each table

Starting points

What do we mean when we say that someone is 'a good listener'?
Think of two people talking. How would you spot 'the good listener'?
Draw out ideas, e.g. doesn't 'butt in', concentrates on what is being said, can repeat, accurately, what has been said.
Who, here, is a good listener? (Choose a volunteer.)
Who, here, is a good talker? (Choose a volunteer.)

ACTIVITIES

1 Interview the 'talker' while the listener concentrates on what is being said. Questions might include:
Where do you live?
Can you tell us about your family?
What do you like doing in your spare time?
What are you 'best' at? 'Worst' at?
What is your most exciting memory? Frightening memory?

After the interview, get the 'listener' to report back as much of what was said as possible and ask:
Has the listener remembered everything? Was anything left out?

Let's try another experiment.

2 Ask for two volunteers to come to each table to write down every sound they hear – inside or outside the hall. Stress, while they do it, that everyone must be **completely still** and **completely silent**. Give them sufficient time.

Closing points

Ask the volunteers to read out their lists.
Which is longer?
Who heard something not mentioned in either of the lists?
Was something read out that no one else noticed?

We often miss things by not really listening.
Let's try to be better listeners today.

The sense of feeling (in more than one sense)

Essential props

▶ A sack (or bin-liner) containing objects, some of which are alike in size and texture*

▶ A pair of sturdy gloves, e.g. boxing gloves, sheepskin mittens

▶ A written list of everything in the sack

*Items to include in sack: pen/pencil/felt-tip, pea/bead, glove/slippers, rubber/plastic ball, die/sugar-lump. Use common materials: wool, felt, cotton, wood, plastic and metal. Include some smaller items: paperclip, thimble, etc.

Starting points

What does 'thick-skinned' or 'thin-skinned' mean?
How can people be 'thick-skinned' or 'thin-skinned'?
Discuss suggestions and explain by talking about sensitive and insensitive behaviour.

How might a sensitive person react when
– a friend is unusually quiet?
– someone in the house has a headache?
– a 'secret' gets out about someone in his or her class?
– a fat person, who is dieting, is caught eating sweets?
Take each question in turn, ask for examples, and comment on them. Repeat the questions to consider insensitive reactions.

Why do we call insensitive people 'thick-skinned'?
Why do we call sensitive people 'thin-skinned?'
Would a thick-skinned person treat others in the same way as a thin-skinned person? How might they be different? (Get ideas.)

ACTIVITIES

Let's try an experiment with feelings of a different kind.
I need two volunteers – one 'thin-skinned' and one 'thick-skinned'!
Choose two. The 'thick-skinned' volunteer must be sent away (perhaps to the secretary's room) until sent for.
The 'thin-skinned' person must rummage through the sack, without looking, and name as many items as possible in a set time. Correct answers can be noted and the score announced.
The 'thick-skinned' volunteer is called in to do the same thing, but this time wearing the sturdy gloves.
Announce the final scores and note the difference between them.

Closing points

Just as gloves stop us feeling with our hands, so a 'thick skin' stops us feeling with our 'hearts' or our emotions.
Which type of person are you: thick-skinned or thin-skinned?

Seeing past your nose

Essential props
- ▶ A mirror
- ▶ A child primed in advance to say what he or she sees in the mirror apart from his or her own reflection

Starting points

What do we mean by 'selfish' people? What do they do
— when they want to eat a sweet without giving any away?
— when someone sees them eating sweets and asks for one?
— when they join in a game of football or netball?
— when they see someone in a mess who needs help?
— when they go to a friend's party and sit down to eat?
— when the poppies come round on Remembrance Day?

Who can tell us about
— something someone did (someone not at this school) that was
*   selfish?* (Stress – **no names**!)
— something someone did that was very unselfish?

ACTIVITIES

Produce a mirror and call children out, one at a time, to say what they see in the mirror. If most of them see their faces, ask what they think of them!
What do you like? What don't you like? (Be supportive!)

Notice how many see anything apart from their own reflection. Make a mental note of what they see.

Make sure that one person has been primed in advance to describe **everything** seen in the mirror **except** 'the face' (i.e. the peripheral reflections).

Ask the children what they notice about these replies.

Closing points

If we look past our noses there's always plenty to see.
Let's see what happens today if we stop looking at ourselves and start looking at others.

Hear here!

Essential props

▶ Two small tables and chairs
▶ Paper and a pencil on each table

Starting points

How much do we hear with our ears? Who can remember what they've heard today? Think of what has happened from the moment you woke up. Does anyone remember a particular sound? Allow time for the children to think. Consider their comments. Try to draw a distinction between what they think they might have heard and what they really heard. Are there any memories of obviously distinctive sounds?

We often miss the sounds around us. What stops us from hearing? Are we
– too busy thinking?
– preoccupied with other things?
– distracted by the 'other' senses?
What are the 'other' senses?

When we concentrate our attention on any particular sense, we often realise how much we normally miss.

Let's think, for a moment, just about what we can hear. I shall need two volunteers who are good at concentrating.
Choose two volunteers and ask them to sit, one at each table.

ACTIVITIES

Sit completely still, and listen to what I shall ask you to do. Everyone can join in, although only you (the volunteers) will be able to write down what you remember. There must be complete stillness.
When everyone is quiet, explain to the volunteers that their first task is to sit still, close their eyes, and listen to every sound, **inside** the room. When you give the word, they jot down what they remember.

When the task has been completed, ask them to do the same again, but this time concentrating only on the sounds **outside** the room.

When the exercise is over, ask them what they felt about the experience and let them read their lists. Comment on differences.

Closing points

Did anyone hear anything, inside or outside, that wasn't mentioned?
Was anyone surprised by the experience? (Can they say why?)
Try, at times during the day, to concentrate on hearing, or any other sense, just for a short while. See what effect concentration has.

Using more than one sense

Essential props
- ▶ A table
- ▶ Foods, disguised by being 'chopped up' or crushed, e.g. apple, carrot, salt, orange-peel, cheese, etc.
- ▶ Four sheets of writing paper and a pencil

Starting points

Would a car work with nothing but an engine?
What else does it need?
Consider how the different parts relate to each other.

Would we be able to walk if our feet had no toes?
Discuss balance.

Could we draw a picture using just our hands?
What else do we use when we draw?
(Eyes? Arms? Joints? Brain? What else?)

Not many things work by themselves. Several parts are involved.
How, for example, would you recognise what you were eating?
(Sight? Taste? One or both? Anything else?)

Let's try some experiments to see just what we use when we do something simple like recognising food.

ACTIVITIES

1 Choose one volunteer to come to the front and taste the foods using all of the senses. The volunteer writes down answers but tells no one. The answers are kept by the leader.

2 Choose a second volunteer to do the same, but this time holding his nose to exclude the sense of smell. Record the results.

3 Choose a third volunteer to repeat the experiment, but with closed eyes. Record the results.

4 The last volunteer does the same again, holding his nose **and** closing his eyes. The results are recorded.

Read out the results, in order, and comment on the differences.

Closing points

Notice, as you do things, which senses you are using.
Are you aware of using more then one sense at any time?
Are there some senses that you use more than others?
Can you develop the ones that you don't often use?

Talking and listening

Essential props ▶ Anything that can be used to create a distraction, e.g. a balloon to inflate and deflate, or a drum to beat

Starting points *People 'communicate' in different ways.*
What do we mean by 'communicate'? Do we have to talk to communicate?
Is it possible to talk to someone without communicating? When?
(Prompt: Talking to a deaf person? Talking in different languages? Talking to someone who isn't listening? Discuss ideas.)
People who talk to each other don't always communicate.

Let's try some experiments to prove it.

ACTIVITIES

1 Ask for two volunteers: a 'talker' and a 'listener'.
Get the 'talker' to describe in detail everything he or she did last weekend. The 'listener' must remember everything and report back.

As soon as the 'talker' begins, distract the 'listener' by inflating and deflating the balloon – or by any other means.

Can the 'listener' report back, or did communications break down? If they did, ask why!

2 Ask for three more 'talkers' to join the volunteers.
Tell each one to think of a question to ask the 'listener'. Allow time to think, then tell them to ask their questions, all together, at the same time, on a given signal. Give the signal!

Can the listener answer every question? If not, why not?

3 Get the 'listener' to ask the 'talkers' for their birth dates and addresses. They must all answer at the same time and together. Do communications break down? If so, why?

Closing points *Very little communication took place for three reasons:*
– Firstly, the listener was distracted.
– Secondly, the listener was questioned by too many people at once.
– Thirdly, the listener was answered by too many people at once.

Today we'll all talk a lot – but will we communicate?
If we don't, can we work out what goes wrong?

Looking for what people say

Essential props ▶ A child chosen before the assembly to be dressed up in bandages and a sling, and primed to answer questions in a certain way (see Starting points, below)

Starting points   *Usually we communicate with each other by talking. But what else do we notice when people talk? Let's see.*

Call out the 'bandaged child' for a rehearsed conversation:
How are you today, 'x'? (Very well, thank you.)
Are you feeling fit and healthy? (Yes, very healthy thank you.)
Good. Has anything happened lately? (No. Nothing unusual!)
Good! I'm pleased. Now, off you go and look after yourself.

Do you think that 'x' was telling the truth?
What did you notice apart from what was said?
Discuss replies, pointing out that when we communicate we have to use our eyes as well as our ears!
What other things can we look for when people talk:
— the expressions on their faces?
— the tone of voice? (Are they sad, happy, bored or excited?)
— the way they stand? (Are they slouched or are they upright?)

If we want to communicate we have to notice all kinds of things.

ACTIVITIES   *Let's think of people's faces: the way they speak and how they stand.*

Ask for three volunteers to demonstrate
— facial expressions, e.g. happiness, sadness, surprise, boredom
— voice tones, e.g. answering cheerfully, miserably, etc.
— body postures, e.g. looking ashamed, angry, afraid, etc.

Use volunteers to demonstrate incongruent responses, e.g.
— sounding cheerful but looking miserable
— answering confidently but looking afraid
— speaking kind words but looking angry.

Closing points   *To communicate we must notice **everything**, not just what people say.*

Making ourselves clear

Essential props
- ▶ Blackboard, easel, chalk and cloth, or equivalent
- ▶ Knowledge of some simple road signs

Starting points

We communicate in lots of ways. How can we communicate apart from talking?
Consider expressions, gestures, art (how?), music (how?), mathematics (diagrams, graphs, signs and symbols — ask for examples).

Emphasise that good communication (in any form) should be simple and clear.

ACTIVITIES

1 Draw some simplified road signs on the blackboard starting with
(a) signs that **warn** (usually inside red **triangles**),
(b) signs that **give orders** (usually in red **circles**), and
(c) signs **giving information** (usually inside **rectangles**).
Get the children to say what each sign means and discuss each one, stressing its **simplicity** and **clarity**.

2 Invite volunteers out to draw their own signs
    (a) from instructions, e.g. Be quiet in the library.
                                Walk in single file.
                                Put litter in bins.
(b) of their own invention. (Invite the other children to guess what they mean.)
Praise **simplicity** and **clarity** whenever it occurs.

Closing points

What would happen if road signs were complicated and confusing? Discuss possibilities.

What happens when people send unclear and muddled messages?

Notice how you communicate today — in writing, drawing, mathematics, speaking, or any other way.
Try to be simple and clear. Let others know what you mean.

Involving people

Essential props
► A small table and three chairs
► Something to be sorted, e.g. a pack of cards, Cuisenaire rods

Starting points

People don't always talk to each other when they meet. Who can think of places where people meet but no one talks (or communicates)? (Doctor's surgery? Buses? Trains?)

Can anyone here remember being somewhere where no one spoke? When? Where? How did you feel?
Discuss and comment.

Whenever we communicate we always involve other people.
— Whom must TV involve if it wants to communicate? (Viewers.)
— Whom must newspapers involve if they want to communicate? (Readers.)
— What about team captains? Teachers? Pop stars? Broadcasters?

In order to communicate, people must involve others.

ACTIVITIES

Let's see what happens to communication when people don't involve each other.

1 Ask for three volunteers. Two are told to sit at the table without doing anything. The third is taken aside and told to 'sort out' what is on the table without speaking to the other two. After a short time, stop the proceedings and ask how each one felt.

*Let's see what happens to communication when people **are** involved.*

2 Re-muddle anything sorted and ask for three more volunteers. Take them aside and appoint a leader who must organise the others so that each has a definite job to do. They can talk to each other while they do it.
Stop the proceedings after an interval and ask how each one felt. (Is there a different response? If so, why?)

Closing points

When people involve each other they have to communicate.
By working together, everyone can have something to do.
Let's try to involve more people today in some of the things we do.

The meaning behind the statement

Essential props ▶ Three crosses (drawn on charts):
1 typical Christian cross
2 'Red Cross' cross (coloured red)
3 'Green Cross Code' cross (coloured green)

Starting points *How do we know what people mean when they talk?*
Think of the word 'holiday'. What does it mean?
Who sees a place they know when I say the word 'holiday'?
Choose two or three children to describe what they picture.

Is everyone's picture of a holiday the same?
Words mean different things to different people.
Let's see what they mean to different people.

ACTIVITIES Ask for three volunteers to come out, listen to the same sentence
and describe what they 'picture'. Give them a sentence, e.g.
The man walked down the street towards a field.
Ask the children to form a clear picture in their minds and to
remember it. Then ask each one, in turn, to describe
– the man (his age, his dress, his appearance, how he walked, etc.)
– the street (What is it like? Is it a particular street?)
– the field (What is in the field? Is it a field they know?)

Try other sentences with different groups of children, e.g.
The vehicle was driven down the lane towards the house.
They stood on the high place and stared at the view.

Try single words, e.g.
flower – group – programme – vegetable.

Use ambiguous words, e.g.
spring – pine – pen – pale (pail) – sea (see) – tail (tale).

Ask what the children think you mean by a 'cross'.
Show each of the three cross charts.
Discuss their different meanings.

Closing points *How do we know what people mean by the words they use?*
Review some of the examples already used.

When you talk to each other, explain yourself clearly.
Ask questions to make sure that others know what you mean.

Misunderstandings

Essential props ▶ None

Starting points *What happens when we 'misunderstand' something? Do we mistake someone's meaning? Grasp 'the wrong end of the stick'?*

What would happen if we misunderstood
— the instructions for making something (a model or a recipe)?
— directions for getting somewhere?
— how to do a sum or solve a problem?
— how to work a machine of some kind?
— how to wire-up a plug or change a fuse?

Who remembers misunderstanding something?
Explore particular instances.

Misunderstandings happen when we think we know something but we don't check it out.

Let's ask some simple questions and see if anyone misunderstands them.

ACTIVITIES Ask volunteers to come out and answer questions, in turn, on different subjects, e.g.
What is an ant? Where would you find one? What do ants do? What do they look like?

When the questions have been asked, explain that you really meant 'aunt' (or aunty) — and ask if the child really thinks that his aunty is an insect that lives underground and stings or, if the child's answers referred to an 'aunt', insist you meant 'ant' and ask if the child really believes that an ant is a woman with a nephew or niece who lives in a house, is five feet odd tall and knits?

Question other children on different subjects, e.g.
What is a leak (leek)? — hair (hare)? — deer (dear)? — beach (beech)? — boy (buoy)?
Where would you find one? etc.
In every case, insist that you wanted the alternative meaning.

Closing points *Make sure that people know what you mean when you speak to them.*
Make sure that you know what they mean when they speak to you.
Make sure that everyone 'knows' — and I don't mean 'nose'! (Point to it.)

Talking to a 'mirror'

Essential props ▶ None

Starting points

What kind of person would we call 'self-centred'?
Listen to ideas and encourage discussion.

How would a self-centred person behave
– buying presents for other people?
– playing with friends?
– listening to someone's problems?

Why do self-centred people find it difficult to communicate? Is it because they never listen or because they only want to talk about themselves? Are there any other reasons?

Let's act out two short scenes. In one I shall act the part of an 'ordinary' person talking to a friend. In the other I shall act the part of a self-centred person talking to a friend. See if you know which is which, and why. I'll need someone to act the friend. (Choose someone.)

ACTIVITIES

1 Ask a series of 'key' questions, and after each one find out more about the answer, e.g.
What is your name? Do you like it? Why/Why not? Who chose it? etc.
Where do you live? Describe the road, your room, etc.
How many people are there in your family? Describe them. Tell me something about each one.
Continue on these lines.

2 Repeat the same 'key' questions, but this time ignore the answers. Talk about your own name, home, family. e.g.
What is your name?
I've got an interesting name too. I was named after . . . etc.
Where do you live?
My house is really lovely. It has three large bedrooms . . . etc.
How many people are there in your family?
My own family is really interesting . . . etc.

Closing points

Which of the two 'questioners' was self-centred? How do you know? Did that person find out much about the other one? Why not?
When we talk today, let's talk to people – not to mirrors!

Rules

Essential props
- A notice (on card) that says 'Do not throw stones at this notice.'
- A die and some counters placed on a table

Starting points
What are rules? (Discuss ideas: Common standards? Laws for everyone?)
What rules do we have in this school? (Ask 'why?' for every one.)
Who has family 'rules'? (Encourage disclosure and discussion.)
What rules are there for everyone? (Discuss laws and reasons for them.)
Are all rules good rules? (Get opinions and encourage discussion.)
Look at this notice! (Show card.) *Is this a good rule? Why? Why not?*
Who can think of other pointless rules? (Debate suggestions.)
Good rules are made for good reasons

ACTIVITIES
*Let's try something with **no** rules.*

1 Ask for two volunteers to come out and play a game together with the die and counters. Don't give them any 'rules'. Stop them after a while. What have they done? Would 'rules' have helped them?

*Let's try again **with** rules.*

2 Ask them to start again but this time give them simple rules, e.g. 'Each player throws the die in turn. A 'three' or a 'six' wins a counter. The winner is the one who collects most.'

3 Invite another pair out to see if they can invent a different game by changing the rules, e.g. 'Players throw the die. Odd numbers collect one counter, even numbers collect two.'

Closing points
Which makes more sense: games with rules or games without them?
Can rules be changed? Have any laws been changed? (e.g. capital and corporal punishment? Were they sensible changes?)
When do we need to change rules? When is it best to keep them?
Think about the 'school rules' – why do we have them?
Are they sensible rules or pointless rules?
What changes in rules or new rules would make this a better school?

Sharing involves giving

Essential props
- ▶ A cake (or bread) and a knife
- ▶ A glass of squash and three straws
- ▶ A candle, a joss-stick and matches

Starting points

When we share, we always give something away.
Who has shared something with someone today?
What did it cost? (What did you have to give?)

What do we have to give when we
— join in someone's game? (Skills? Co-operation?)
— share some sweets? (The sweets!)
— visit someone who is old or sick? (Our time?)
— help someone to do something difficult? (Effort? Energy? Ideas?)

When we share, do we ever get back what we give? Can we
— get back our sweets from someone who's eaten them?
— get back the time we spend when we play a game or help
*   someone?*

If we don't give something, we can't share anything.
Let's see what we have to give to make sharing worth while.

ACTIVITIES

Ask three volunteers to share the cake without eating it.
Was it worth sharing? What do they need to do?
Let them eat the cake!

Ask three more to share the straws without drinking the squash.
Were the straws worth sharing? Why not?
Let them drink!

Ask children to come and share the candle without lighting it.
Can they? What must they do to share its light?
Light the candle for them. Let everyone watch the flame.

Invite children out to share the joss-stick without lighting it.
Can they?
Light it for them. How many others are 'sharing' the scent?

Closing points

If we don't give something away we can't share anything.
What happened to the cake, the squash, the candle, the joss-stick?
*Could we have shared them **and** kept them?*
Would there have been any point in keeping any of them anyway?

Sharing the load

Essential props   ▶ Two pairs of scissors
▶ Two pieces of squared paper

Starting points   *What is a 'community'? (Encourage discussion.)*
A group? A town? A city? A country? A school?

How do communities work? (Consider the different 'roles'.)
– In a town? (The 'services' and what they do.)
– In a family? (Different tasks and how they are shared.)
– In a school? (The roles: teachers, cook, cleaners, etc.)
– In class? ('Monitors' – who is one? What jobs do they do?)

Are there times when we can share jobs in a community? When might we
– have to 'nurse'? (When someone is hurt in the playground?)
– have to be a 'caretaker'? (When someone spills something?)

Sometimes, instead of saying 'that's his job' or 'that's her job', we have to do 'other people's' jobs.

ACTIVITIES   *Let's imagine a typical classroom at the end of the day. Billy and Mary have been having a wonderful time cutting out thousands of tiny squares.*
Ask for two volunteers, 'Billy' and 'Mary', to cut up their pieces of paper and let all the bits drop on the floor. Explain that in this class there is a clearing-up monitor! Choose a clearing-up monitor to come to the front. Ask:
Whose job is it to clear up?
Encourage debate but insist that the monitor clears up. Stop the monitor after a while and ask if there is a fairer and quicker way. After discussion, insist that 'Billy' and 'Mary' clear up. Stop them after a while and ask if there might be an even better way. Could the class (or whole community) help?
Ask the 'front row' to be 'the class' and let them **all** help.

Closing points   *Jobs don't take long when everyone helps.*
Notice what happens today when your class clears up.
How many people say 'That's not my job'?
Try doing something that 'isn't your job', and see how much time it saves.

Belonging to a group

Essential props
- ▶ A sheet of paper
- ▶ A telephone directory
- ▶ A single (breakable) stick
- ▶ An (unbreakable) bundle of sticks

Starting points

People often join groups. Do any of you belong to groups out of school?
Choose people to describe
— the group;
— when and where it meets;
— what happens when it meets;
— what they like about belonging to the group.

What different kinds of group do we have in school?
Get as many different suggestions as possible, e.g.
— Clubs? 'Houses'? Teams? Gangs?
— Why do children belong to them?
— What do they like about belonging?

Groups are stronger than people on their own. They can change things that people on their own couldn't change.
People in groups can change laws. What laws would you like to change?
People in groups can improve where they live. What would you improve?
Groups are always stronger than individuals.

Look what happens in this experiment!

ACTIVITIES

1 Call out volunteers, one at a time, to
   (a) tear up a piece of paper
(b) tear up the telephone directory
(c) snap a single stick
(d) snap a 'bundle' of sticks.

2 Ask for someone to sing a song (known to the school) alone!
Ask a group to sing it together! (Is there a different response?)

Closing points

When we join together in groups we feel much stronger.
Think of the directory, the sticks, and the 'choir'.
If you don't belong to a group, is there one that you could join?
Notice how much more you can do when you're part of a group.

Discord and harmony

Essential props ▶ The first five notes of the scale *doh ray me fah* and *soh* (use the notes G A B C and D on chime-bars or – if you have players – recorders or other melodic instruments)

Starting points
What is 'harmony'?
Hear suggestions and prompt with questions:
How would a choir sound singing in harmony, or an orchestra playing in harmony? How would we know if they weren't in harmony?

How could we describe something not in harmony? (Jarring? Clashing?) Ask for ideas. Introduce the idea of 'concord' and 'discord'.

What do we mean when we say a community 'lives in harmony'? (Working together? Contributing different skills towards common ends? Fitting in with each other? Helping each other?) Ask for ideas.

Communities can live in harmony or in discord. Which is better?

ACTIVITIES
Ask for five volunteers. Each is to play only one note on one of the instruments. (If recorder players or other instrumentalists are used, make sure they can play one of the five notes named above.)
Ask each player, in turn, to play a short tune on the one note.
Can we have harmony if only one player plays at a time?

Ask them to play together, each on the note selected and all at the same time.
Did that sound harmonious? Why not? How can we make it sound better?

Ask for notes G B and D to be played together.
Ask for notes A and C to be played together.
Ask each group to play together, alternately in turn.

Closing points
There is harmony when the right things happen at the right time. Everyone can be involved, but not all at the same time. Notice how well the people you work and play with mix together. Think about your own contribution. How and when can you help your group?

Variety in numbers

Essential props ▶ The words of the following rhyme:

'1, 2, 3, 4, 5, once I caught a fish alive.
6, 7, 8, 9, 10, then I put it back again.
Why did you let it go? Because it bit my finger so.
Which finger did it bite? This little finger on the right!'

These words, either duplicated or projected, must be capable of being read by ten children facing the assembly.

Starting points *Communities provide us with 'variety'. What is 'variety'? Describe the 'various' things that you might find at school – in a holiday camp – in the town centre – at a fairground.*
We find variety where people meet, and variety in the people themselves. Think of all the various people here!
Discuss the variety: looks, personalities, mannerisms, etc.

People together make life more colourful. Let me show you what I mean.

ACTIVITIES *I need someone who can read (or recite) a short rhyme.*
Choose a volunteer to learn it by rote (or read it through) before reciting it to the rest. Praise the attempt, but then ask:
Could we use our community, or the people in it, to present the rhyme in an even more varied and interesting way?
Encourage ideas before making the following proposal:
Let's use ten people instead of one and try out this idea:
Number each child (1–10) and divide the whole group into two subgroups: group A (1–5) and group B (6–10).

Rehearse and perform the rhyme in the following way:
'1 2 3 4 5' (each number spoken by the person whose number it is)
'Once I caught a fish alive.' (spoken by group A)
'6 7 8 9 10' (each number spoken by the person whose number it is)
'Then I put it back again.' (group B)
'Why did you let it go?' (A) *'Because it bit my finger so.'* (B)
'Which finger did it bite?' (A) *'This little finger on the right!'* (B)

Closing points *All communities can use their members in various ways.*
We can enjoy the variety we have by making the best use we can of each other.

Second chances

Essential props   ▶   Blackboard, easel, chalk and cloth, or equivalent

Starting points   *Some games never go out of fashion.*
What games do you play that your parents played as children?
Listen to suggestions and comment on them.

Why do certain games stay in fashion? What makes a game 'good'?
(Excitement? Competition? Team work and co-operation?)

Games often 'act out' what happens in real life.
Let's think about something that happens in real life and see who
can think of a game that acts it out.

Has anyone 'messed up' the first page of a new exercise book?
Get examples. Ask what happened.
What can you do if you make a mistake in a new book?
Get suggestions, e.g. Get another book.
How many 'second chances' should you get?
Discuss and debate the replies. Who would pay for the new books?
What can you do with a rubber if you make a mistake?
Consider replies, e.g. Rub it out.
What would happen if you rubbed out the same mistake several
times?
Suggest possibilities, e.g. a hole would appear in the paper.

Stress: *There is usually a limit to the number of chances we have.*

ACTIVITIES   *Is there a game that gives us a limited number of second chances?*
Listen to ideas. Congratulate anyone who suggests 'Hangman'.
Choose a group to play 'Hangman' on the blackboard in front of
the school.
Comment on everything that happens as it happens.

Closing points   Compare the game with real life, e.g.
What happens at first when you make mistakes? (More chances?)
What happens as you get things right? (Things begin to make
sense?)
What happens if you keep making mistakes? (Chances run out?)
Is life like that?

Let's notice how many second chances we get today – and see if we
use them wisely or end up by 'hanging' ourselves.

Winning, losing and stalemate

Essential props ▶ Blackboard, easel, chalk and cloth, or equivalent

Starting points

Sometimes we can't win or lose. Think about this:
If I said 'School is really good', would I be right?
Who thinks school is good?
Who doesn't think that school is good?
Who thinks there's no way of winning the argument? Why not?
Some arguments can't be won or lost because there's no right answer.

But . . . (point to the blackboard)
What would happen if I argued, 'This is not a blackboard'?
Could I win or lose that argument?
Who thinks it is a blackboard?
Who thinks it isn't a blackboard?
Who thinks it would be a waste of time to argue about it? Why?

Some things are either right or wrong. There's no point in arguing.
We win or lose, or we don't get anywhere. Who can think of games like that?
Listen to suggestions and comment on them, e.g. football (win, lose or draw), chess (win, lose or stalemate).

ACTIVITIES

Let's play a game that we can only win, or lose, or get nowhere.
Invite pairs out to play 'Noughts and crosses'.

Play as many games as it takes to illustrate the point.
If no one 'draws', direct a game to illustrate 'stalemate', e.g.

1st player	*centre*	2nd player	*top left*
1st player	*bottom left*	2nd player	*top right*
1st player	*top centre*	2nd player	*bottom centre*
1st player	*centre right*	2nd player	*centre left*
1st player	*stalemate!*		

Closing points

Listen to the arguments that come up today.
Are they straightforward arguments, like 'Noughts and crosses', with winners and losers, or could there be more than one answer?
If there could be, can you say something to help sort things out?

Sharing the limelight

Essential props ▶ None

Starting points
The games we play are often like the things we do in real life.

Some games remind us that we often win or lose.
What games depend on winning and losing?
When, in real life, do we win or lose? (Get concrete examples.)

Other games remind us that we sometimes get several chances when we make mistakes.
What games offer several chances? (Twenty questions? Others?)
When, in life, do we get several chances? (Warnings? Near accidents?)

Some games give us a chance to be the 'centre of attraction'.
When would we say that someone is the 'centre of attraction'?
(When they are being noticed?)
Can you think of people who are often the 'centre of attraction'?
(Brides? Bridesmaids? Actors? Football stars? Pop stars?)
Can anyone here remember being the 'centre of attraction'?
(When? What were you doing? How did you feel?)
Has anyone been jealous of someone who was the 'centre of attraction'? (Can you tell us about it?)
Most people, even shy people, like to be the centre of attraction sometimes.

Let's play a game that gives everyone a chance to be the 'centre of attraction'. Can anyone guess what the game will be?

ACTIVITIES
Play 'I Spy' (perhaps with a selected group, e.g. 1st or 4th years). Choose one child to start, and call each right-guesser out to the front in turn.

Closing points
Not all games are about winning or losing.
*This game is about **sharing**. Anyone can win. There are several winners.*
Every winner gets a chance to be the centre of attraction.
Notice how you feel when you're the centre of attraction. Do you enjoy it?
If you do, can you think of ways to let other people enjoy it?
Which is more fun: to be the centre of attraction yourself, or to find ways of letting someone else be the centre of attraction?

Chance

Essential props
- ▶ A strip of card divided into 10 squares (1 × 10)
- ▶ A die
- ▶ Two counters (different colours)

Starting points

Sometimes we succeed because we work at something and learn the skills.

What skills do we learn at school? (Reading? Writing? Football, Netball? Painting? Drawing?)

Who's good at something that was very difficult to learn? What? Can you tell us what you found difficult? How (and when) did you start to get over the difficulties?

Some of us find we have natural skills. Who's good at something that just came naturally? What? How did you discover you were good at it?

Sometimes we have to work for what we get. Sometimes we get things by chance. Who can think of something good that happened to them just by chance? Get children to talk about 'lucky' times — unexpected good fortune. *Are things that happen by chance always good? Who's been unlucky? What happened?*

Sometimes we have to work for what we get. Sometimes we get things by chance. Some games need a lot of skill, but others are based on chance. Get some examples.

Watch this game. Is it a game of skill or a game of chance?

ACTIVITIES

Ask for two players.
Explain that the aim is for each player to move a counter along the strip of card from square 1 to square 10. The die determines the number of 'moves'. Each player takes it in turns to throw.

Closing points

Was the winner more skilful than the loser? Could the loser have improved by practising or by working harder?

Chance plays a part in everyone's life. Which do you prefer — working for success, or getting it by chance?

Imagining other states of being

Essential props
- ► A blindfold
- ► A rag for a three-legged race
- ► An apple floating in a bowl of water

Starting points

Some games help us to understand what life would be like if we didn't have the things that we normally take for granted.
There are several things that we often take for granted until something happens to make us think.
What might happen to make us realise how much we need
– our friends? (Quarrels? Moving away? Being left out?)
– our families? (Mum, dad, brother or sister going away?)
– our health? (An illness or accident? A sudden headache?)
Get the children to talk about their own experiences.
When everything's going well we take things for granted.
Who can think of any games where we have to manage without the things that we normally take for granted?
Discuss examples.

Ask for volunteers to play the games described below.

ACTIVITIES

1 Get the apple from the water using only the mouth.

Does it teach us how much we rely on our hands?
Ask those who take part to talk about their reactions.

2 Have a three-legged race.

How does it feel? What was awkward or difficult?

3 Use the blindfold to play a game like 'Blind Man's Buff' or 'Squeak Piggy Squeak'.

How did the blindfolded person feel?

Closing points

Games like these, as well as being fun, can help us to understand how it feels to be without things we usually take for granted.
Imagine how it would be without some of the things we take for granted.
Play these games and notice how you feel.
Think of other games like them and try them out.

Testing our limits

Essential props
- ▶ Three balls or bean-bags
- ▶ A hoop
- ▶ A football

Starting points

When someone 'pushes himself or herself to the limit', what does he or she do?
Listen to ideas and invite comments.

How would these people 'push themselves to the limit'?
– Someone wanting to catch a bus that's about to leave
– A short person in a crowd who wants to see a football match
– Someone who is late for work (or school)
– A person who wants to lose weight
– Someone with a lot of work to finish by a deadline

*When do people **have** to 'push themselves to the limit'?*
Listen to examples and discuss them.

Who can remember times when they've 'pushed themselves to the limit'?
Listen to examples and discuss them.

We sometimes play games to test our limits.
What games do we play to test our limits? (Discuss replies.)
Let's try some.

ACTIVITIES

Ask for volunteers to try the following exercises. Time different children.

1 Keep first one ball (or bean-bag) – then two and then three – in the air for as long as possible.

2 Keep a hoop spinning around the waist for as long as possible.

3 Keep a football under control for as long as possible, e.g. bouncing it into the air from the toe, or knee, or head.
Get the children to suggest their own challenges.

Closing points

There are times in life when we have to push ourselves to the limit.
Recall some examples from 'Starting points'.

Try pushing yourselves to the limit today. See if you can break your own records.

Survival

Essential props
▶ A record player or tape recorder with a record or tape of some light music
▶ Five chairs (set out for a game of 'Musical Chairs')

Starting points
Games often show us what real life is like, and one thing that we all have to do, in life, is **stay alive***! We call it 'surviving'.*

When might people have to struggle to survive?
Encourage discussion: After an accident? During serious illness? At birth? Being lost in the desert? Mountaineering? Exploring? Promote ideas and listen to any tales of survival that the children might know from their own real-life experience.

What famous stories are based on tales of survival?
'Swiss Family Robinson'? 'ET'? Can the children summarise any?

What might we do to survive
— in tests? (Revise beforehand? Any other ideas?)
— when a bully is after us? (Face-up to the bully? Run for our lives?)
— when we're 'caught in the act'? (Own up? Make excuses?)

People survive in different ways.

There are games that act out 'survival'. Let's see how different people manage to survive.

ACTIVITIES

1 Play 'Musical Chairs'. Ask for six volunteers. The players walk round the chairs while the music plays, and sit when it stops. A chair is removed each time the game re-starts, until two players are left to compete for the last chair. What do the children notice about the survivor's behaviour?

2 Play 'O'Grady Says'. Choose seven volunteers. One is the leader whose commands (touch your heads — your toes — your right ear — etc.) must be obeyed only when prefixed by the phrase 'O'Grady says'. Players who obey when the phrase is omitted drop out until only one survivor is left.

Closing points
Think of other games that are based on 'survival'.
What do they teach you about your own survival techniques?
Are there times when 'survival at all costs' is not the best thing?
Can you think of people who did something good by choosing not to survive in the normal way?

Difference and uniqueness

Essential props
► Blackboard, easel and chalk, or equivalent
► Headings written on board (see Activities below)

Starting points
*Are any two things in the universe **exactly** alike?*
Discuss responses. What is the general consensus? What minute differences might there be between apparently identical objects, e.g. two prints or two objects from the same mould?

One of the strangest mysteries is that no two things are exactly alike. Everything is unique. What is 'unique'?

Sometimes similar things look the same. Would human beings look alike to an alien? How do human beings look alike?

ACTIVITIES
Ask for three volunteers.

Look at these three perfect humans. How are they all alike? (Two eyes – arms – hands – legs – feet? Ten 'fingers'? One head -- nose – neck – head of hair? Anything else?)

At first, humans might look alike. But let's look more carefully.

Ask for another volunteer, an 'alien'.
Who thinks we might find three humans with the same-coloured hair? Eyes?
Ask the 'alien' to call out the colour-details (light or dark) of the three 'humans', and write them down under these headings (already prepared on the board):

Human's name	Eye colour	Hair colour

Are any two humans alike? How are they different?
Discuss physical differences (height, build, colouring, etc.), differences in temperament (excitability, cheerfulness, etc.), and differences in likes and dislikes (food, music, hobbies, etc.).

Closing points
Could we ever describe everything that makes people different? Notice how you're different from others and how they're different from you. No two people are alike in every way. Everyone is **unique**.

Endless possibility

Essential props

▶ Six pencils
▶ Twelve sheets of paper

Starting points

Who knows what my next sentence will be? Can anyone know?

Who knows what I shall write on this paper? (Hold up a blank sheet.)
No one knows. You'd have to guess.

Who knows what they'll be doing in an hour from now?
No one knows about the future.

What could happen now?
– Something unexpected? (Any ideas?)
– Something that distracts us? (Who's daydreaming now?)

Life is full of possibilities. Every day we can decide what we shall do.
Even in lessons we can switch on, switch off, try, or give up.

ACTIVITIES

1 Ask for six volunteers who can write quite quickly. Give each one a pencil and paper. Ask them to write down their favourite colour, TV programme, food, drink, sweets, hobby, toy. *Can anyone know for certain what each one decided to write? There are endless possibilities. Let's be nosy and find out.* Get the children to read out their answers in turn.

2 Ask for six more 'quick writers' to come and play Consequences. They can sit in a circle on the floor to fill in the missing words as you read a story. After each word they fold their papers over and pass them on. Example:

'(Name of pop star) *went to tea with* (name of teacher or head). *They ate* (a favourite meal), *played* (favourite game) *and went for a swim in a pool filled with* (favourite drink). *When the evening was over they played with their* (favourite toy).'

Let's see what happened.
Get the children to call out, in turn, what they wrote, as you read the story again.

Closing points

Life is filled with endless possibilities.
How do people make your life more interesting?
What harmless things can you do to make their lives more interesting?

Infinity

Essential props
- ▶ A hoop
- ▶ A large ball
- ▶ A bean bag

Starting points

Life is full of mysteries.
We say that everything has a beginning and end. But does it?
Who can think of something that does have a beginning and end?
(Days? Roads? People's lives? Journeys? A piece of string?)
Listen to ideas and encourage discussion, e.g. Do roads end?

Who can think of anything that doesn't have a beginning or an end?
(Time? Space? A series of numbers, negative to positive?)
Discuss suggestions. Promote debate.

Does anyone know a word for something that has no beginning or end?

Some ideas, like infinity, seem hard to understand.
Let's do some simple things that might help us to understand.

ACTIVITIES

1 Choose a child to hold a hoop and feed it through both hands until the hoop comes to an end.
Can it be done? Why not?

2 Choose a child to hold a ball. Ask where the surface of the ball begins and ends.
Is the question pointless? Why?

3 Choose three children to play a relay, passing a bean-bag back over their heads. The child at the back always comes to the front and repeats the procedure.
Will the game ever end? If someone came in while the game was in progress, could they tell where it had started?

Closing points

We often think that everything has a beginning and an end. But does it?
– What follows Winter? Spring? Summer? Autumn? And then?
– Where do flowers come from? Where do seeds come from?
– Which came first: the oak or the acorn, the chicken or the egg?

*Some people say that there is nothing after death. Can anyone be sure? What do **you** think?*

Creation

Essential props
- ► Two pictures (reproductions of paintings by different artists)
- ► Two different plants (or flowers)
- ► Blackboard, easel, chalk and cloth, or equivalent

Starting points

When people create things, what do they do?
Listen to suggestions. Prompt if necessary, e.g. make things, write stories, draw pictures.

Has anyone created something today?
Encourage discussion.

What can we create with our faces? (Different expressions?)
Choose volunteers to create expressions (happy, sad, sulky, etc.).
Who likes creating funny faces?
Have a 'funny face competition'. Draw attention to the 'creation' of laughter.

Different creations often come from similar starting points. We've just seen that similar faces create different expressions.
Show the two paintings.
Both artists used similar materials – but look at the differences!
How are they different? (Subject? Colour? Texture? Mood?)

Show the plants (or flowers).
These came from similar bulbs/seeds. But look how different they are!
Discuss the differences (size, leaf-shape, petals, etc.).

Let's see what different people can create from the same things.

ACTIVITIES

1 Write the words, 'I can go' on the board.
Can anyone re-arrange these words to create a different meaning?
Explain that punctuation marks can be added.

2 Write the numbers 1, 2 and 3 on the board.
How many different combinations of the same numbers can be created? Any guesses?
Let someone try, e.g. 123 231 312 321 132 213.

Closing points

Everything you think, say or do is an act of creation.
Think about what you 'create' today. How inventive can you be?

Transformation

Essential props
- ▶ A large square sheet of paper
- ▶ A pair of scissors
- ▶ A bulb and a flowering pot plant that has been grown from a bulb (useful, but not essential)

Starting points

What do we mean when we say that something or someone is 'transformed'?
Listen to answers and introduce the concept of complete change by using examples. For example:
What happened to the Frog in the fable when the Princess kissed it?
Invite someone who knows the story to tell it.
What happens to a bulb?
Show them the bulb and plant if you have them.
What happens to a chrysalis?
Let children describe the process.

What happened to the Frog, the bulb and the chrysalis are all examples of how things can be transformed. Can anyone think of any other examples?
Encourage responses and invite reactions.

When something or someone is transformed, it always seems like a mystery. Let's try something simple that always makes people look twice.

ACTIVITIES

Ask for a volunteer to fold the paper, in four stages, always from corner **a** to corner **b** (see diagrams).

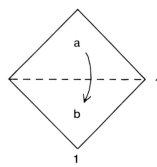
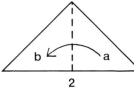

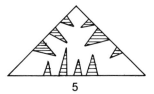

Snip out the shaded parts (stage 5) and, finally, open it up and show everyone.

Closing points

A plain sheet of paper was transformed into something different. Look for other examples today, for example cloudy skies into sunny blue skies.
Is there something about yourself that you'd like to see transformed?

Unseen forces

Essential props
- ▶ Any article or object that can be dropped
- ▶ An empty box or basket
- ▶ A candle (and a means of lighting it)
- ▶ A glass or jar that fits over the candle

Starting points
There are things around us that we use but never see.
Hold up the article and ask:
What will happen if I let go of this?
Drop it and ask:
Why did it fall? What 'pulled' it to the ground? (Mention 'gravity'.)
What would happen to us without gravity?
Hear suggestions and discuss the possibilities: floating into space, etc. Repeat the opening idea:
There are things all around us that we use but cannot see.
Who can think of some other examples?
Encourage ideas, e.g. breathing air, receiving love and care.

ACTIVITIES
Call for volunteers to demonstrate the effects of the 'invisible' by performing the following feats (with as much help and supervision from the leader as seem necessary).

1. Place the article (dropped earlier) into the box or basket and 'spin' it through a vertical circle to show that it doesn't fall out. (It might be wise to practise first!)
What invisible force keeps it there? (Discuss centrifugal force.)

2. Light the candle and get a child, standing as far from the candle as possible, to blow out the flame.
What touched the flame that no one saw?

3. Light the candle and cover it with the inverted jar or glass.
Why does the flame go out? What does it need to burn?
Point out that flames need just enough air — not too much and not too little. Is it the same with people and affection?

Closing points
There are mysteries around us that we never see.
We only know they're there because of their effects.
Let's open our eyes to the things we can't see!

Quiet moments

Essential props ▶ None

Starting points Our minds are always racing with thoughts.

What are you thinking about now? Were you
– listening to what I was saying?
– thinking about something else that was happening around you?
– daydreaming? (Where were you? What were you dreaming about?)

Try to imagine **not thinking**. Sit still and try **not to think**!

What happened? Who can tell us what happened when you tried not to think?
Listen to any who offer accounts. Did others find the same?

It's almost impossible **not** to think, but there are ways of slowing down our thoughts. Let's try some.

Let three volunteers come and sit with the others at the front (amongst them rather than apart from them).

ACTIVITIES I want everyone (and in particular our volunteers) to sit quite still and focus on anything in front of them.

Take plenty of time and pause between each of the following suggestions:
Look really carefully at what is in front of you. Look at its colour – its different shades – how the light falls on it – where it is darkest – and lightest – how it might feel. Look at every part.

When you're ready, try closing your eyes. Imagine you can still see it: think of its colour – its different shades – the light falling on it. Keep thinking about it. Don't be distracted.
When you are ready, open your eyes.

Ask the volunteers what happened. Did they enjoy it? Was it easy? Were they distracted? By what? What was good about the experience? Which were the easy or difficult parts of the exercise?

Closing points Sometimes it helps to find quiet moments in the middle of busy days. When your mind is racing around, relax, and think about just one thing. There are mysteries everywhere – if we take the time to look.